The Classical Piano
Sheet Music Series

CHRISTMAS
CAROL
ARRANGEMENTS

ISBN 978-1-70516-827-1

Visit Hal Leonard Online at
www.halleonard.com

World headquarters, contact:
Hal Leonard
7777 West Bluemound Road
Milwaukee, WI 53213
Email: info@halleonard.com

In Europe, contact:
Hal Leonard Europe Limited
1 Red Place
London, W1K 6PL
Email: info@halleonardeurope.com

In Australia, contact:
Hal Leonard Australia Pty. Ltd.
4 Lentara Court
Cheltenham, Victoria, 3192 Australia
Email: info@halleonard.com.au

Contents

Away in a Manger

Traditional
Words by John T. McFarland (v. 3)
Music by William J. Kirkpatrick

Andante con moto

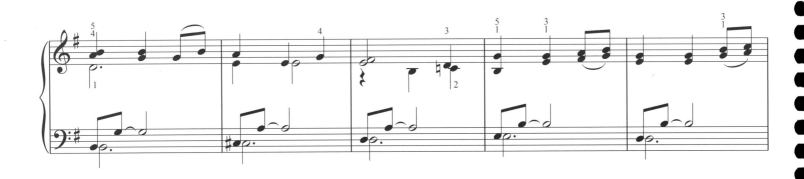

Bring a Torch, Jeannette, Isabella

17th Century French Provençal Carol

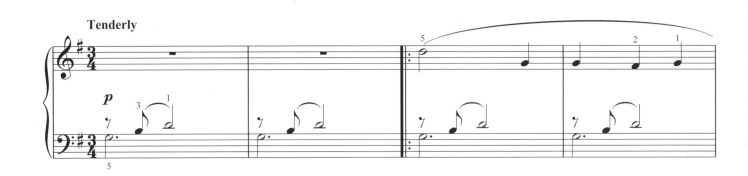

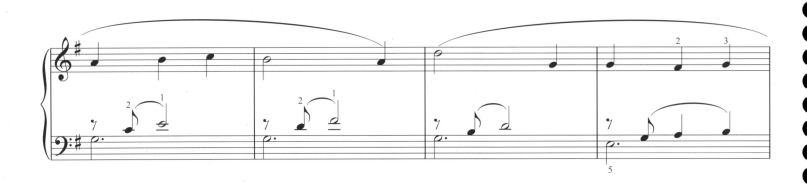

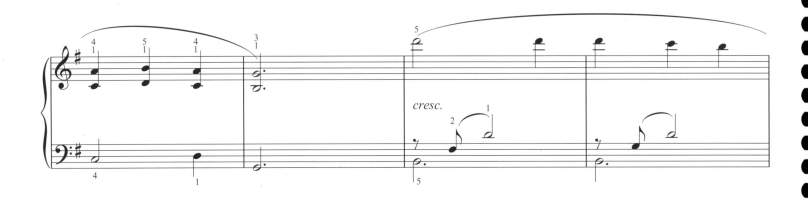

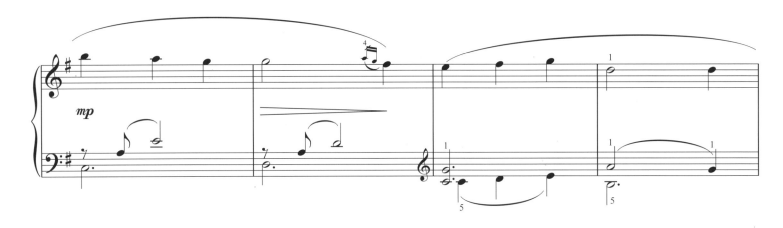

Coventry Carol

Traditional Carol

Deck the Hall

Traditional Welsh Carol

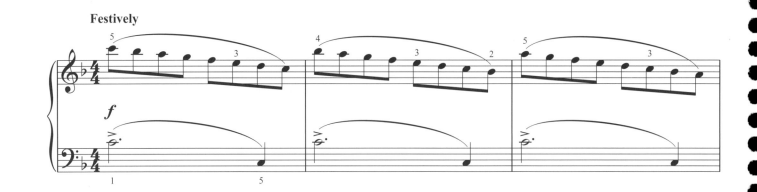

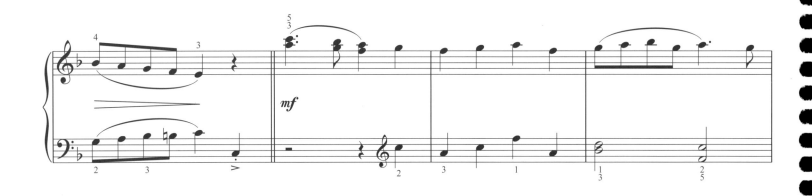

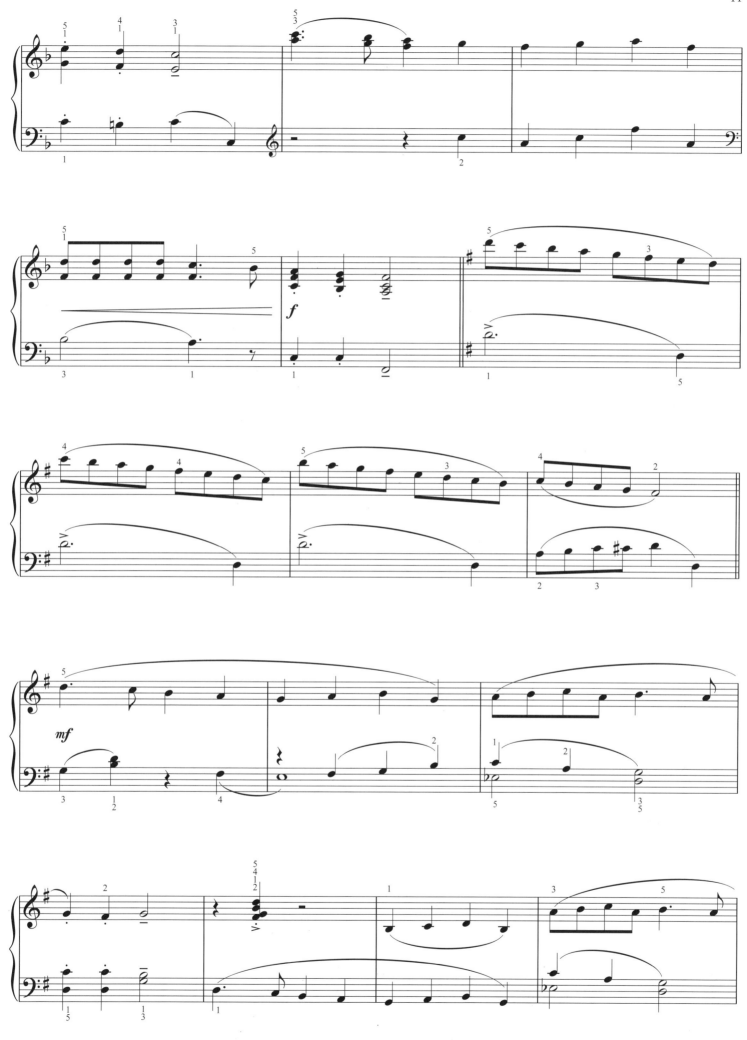

The First Noel

17th Century English Carol
Music from W. Sandys' *Christmas Carols*

God Rest Ye Merry, Gentlemen

Traditional English Carol

Moderately slow

mp

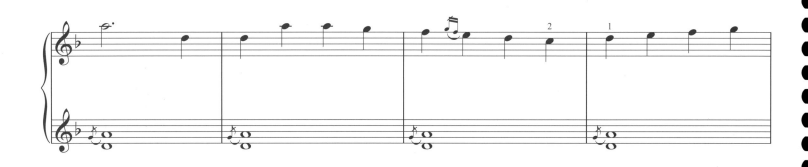

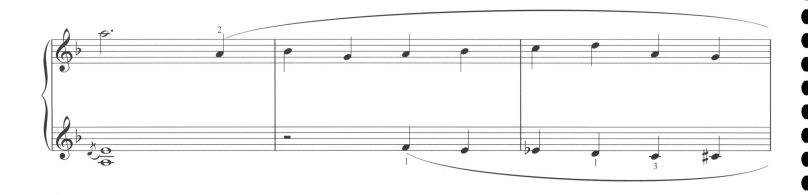

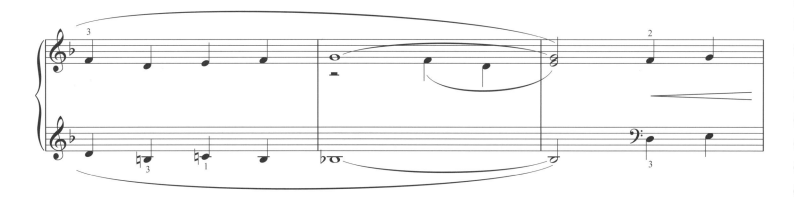

O Come, All Ye Faithful

Music by John Francis Wade
Latin Words translated by Frederick Oakeley

Gently flowing, in two

Hark! The Herald Angels Sing

Words by Charles Wesley
Music by Felix Mendelssohn-Bartholdy

He Is Born

Traditional French Carol

In dulci jubilo

14th Century German Melody

Moderately fast ♩. = c. 84

In the Bleak Midwinter

Poem by Christina Rossetti
Music by Gustav Holst

Infant Holy, Infant Lowly

Traditional Polish Carol

Joy to the World

Words by Isaac Watts
Music by George Frideric Handel

O Come, O Come Emmanuel

Plainsong, 13th Century
Words translated by John M. Neale
and Henry S. Coffin

Andante con moto ♩ = c. 128

O Holy Night

French Words by Placide Cappeau
English Words by John S. Dwight
Music by Adolphe Adam

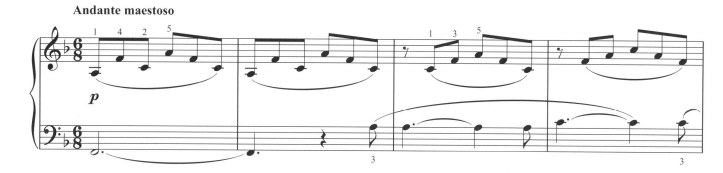

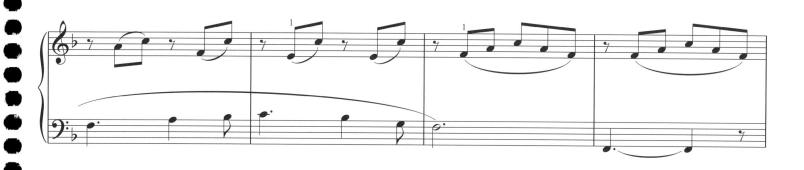

Once in Royal David's City

Words by Cecil F. Alexander
Music by Henry J. Gauntlett

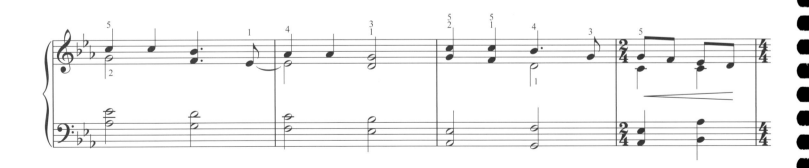

Silent Night

Words by Joseph Mohr
Translated by John F. Young
Music by Franz X. Gruber

More motion

mp

cresc.

Still, Still, Still

Salzburg Melody, c.1819
Traditional Austrian Text

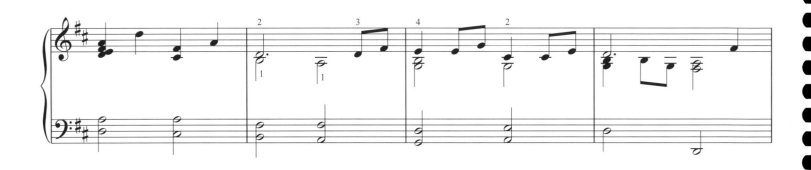

Sussex Carol

Traditional English Carol

Allegretto

What Child Is This?

Words by William C. Dix
16th Century English Melody

Andante con moto ♩. = 50-58